Blend Hunt

Set 5

Written by Kassi Gilmour

Practise the sounds

m s t a p i f c r o d h
e n g k ck u l ll ss ff b j
w wh y th sh v qu z zz x
ch ng oo oo th

The Blend Hunt books are designed to help children practise blending new sounds within each set. Once each word is successfully blended, children search for the item that matches the words they have read on each page.

Practise tricky words

to they of are have all her day
for like said what want saw be
were one some come

Blend Hunt

Set 5

Written by Kassi Gilmour

| b | oo | t |

| d | r | e | ss |

| b | e | n | ch |

cook   chips

think

shops chop truck

moon roof shed

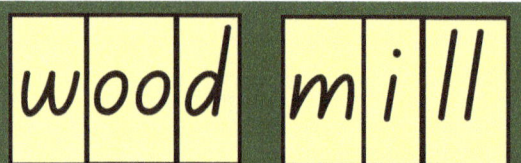

pool block flip

| shr | u | b | l | oo | k | b | oo | t | s |

zoo baboon croc

lunch box

thongs

Sing

Written by Kassi Gilmour

Practise the sounds

u l ll ss ff b j w wh y
th sh v qu z zz x
ch ng oo oo th

Practise blending sounds

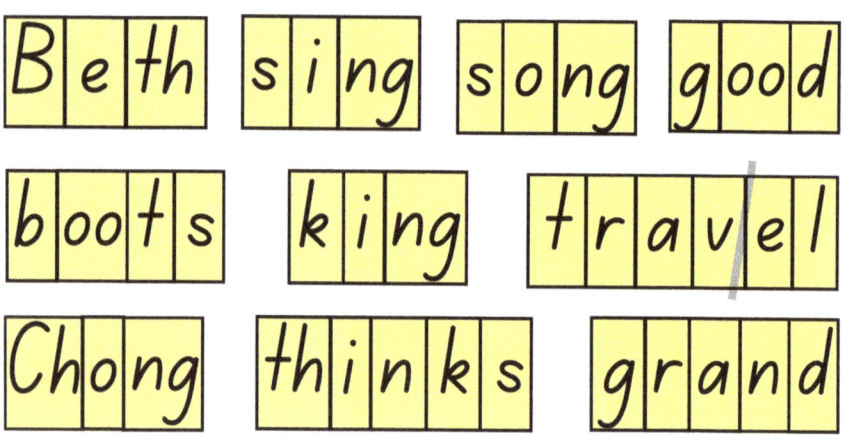

Practise tricky words

to too they of are have all h<u>all</u>
her day for like said what want
saw be were one some come

Sing

Set 5

Written by Kassi Gilmour

Beth likes to sing.

She is good at it, too.

With her best dress on, she slips on her boots.

Beth will sing for the king of Chong.

They travel to the king's grand hall.

Ding! Dong! The bells ring.

Beth steps up to sing.

She sings her song.

The king claps his hands.
"That was good," he said.

Beth was glad and felt like a champ.

"Thank you, king," she said.

Beth thinks this is the best day she has had.

Questions:

1. What does Beth like to do?
2. Where is she going?
3. Does the king like her singing?
4. How does Beth feel about her performance?
5. Have you ever performed for an audience?

Cook

Written by Kassi Gilmour

Practise the sounds

u l ll ss ff b j w wh y
th sh v qu z zz x
ch ng oo oo th

Practise blending sounds

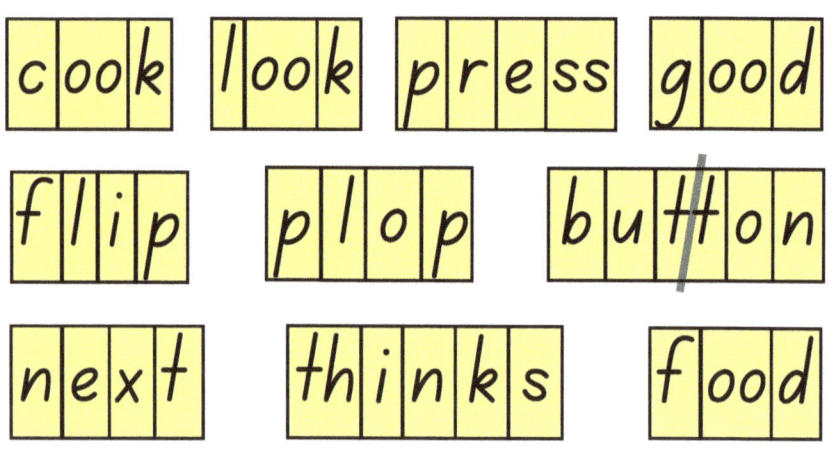

Practise tricky words

to into they of are have all her
day for like said what want saw
be were one some come

Cook

Set 5

Written by Kassi Gilmour

I like food.

I want to be a cook one day.

I will cook for my mum.

Get a pan and press the 'on' button.

Crack the eggs.

Tip the milk in.

Mix the eggs and milk well.

Check if the pan is hot.

When the pan is hot, tip the mix into it.

Let it cook.

Next, cook the buns.

Up pop the buns.

Flip the eggs in the pan.

Press the 'off button.

Plop the eggs on the bun.

The food looks yum!

I tell mum to come in for her eggs.

Mum thinks I will be a good cook one day.

Questions:

1. What does the boy do?
2. Why does he dream of being a chef?
3. Why do you think he wanted to cook for his mum?
4. Retell the instructions for cooking eggs on toasted buns.
5. Have you ever helped with cooking?

The Woods

Written by Kassi Gilmour

Practise the sounds

u l ll ss ff b j w wh y
th sh v qu z zz x
ch ng oo oo th

Practise blending sounds

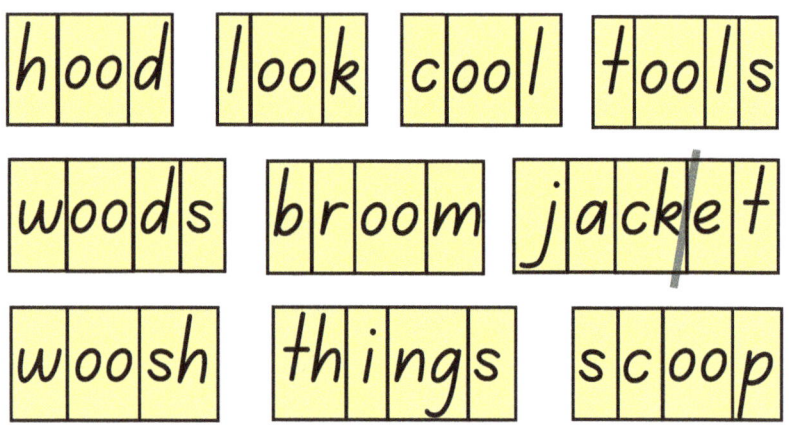

Practise tricky words

they of are have all sm<u>all</u> her to
day today for like said what want
saw be were one some come

The Woods

Set 5

Written by Kassi Gilmour

I am Jess.

I have a small red hood on my jacket.

It is good for cool days.

Today is cool, and I am off to Nan's hut.

It is a long stroll in the woods to Nan's hut.

I have some food for her in my pack.

I set off.

Woosh! What was that in the shrub?

I look and spot long fangs.

It is the Big Bad Fox!

I have to think quick.

I run on the quick track to the wood mill.

The Big Bad Fox saw me have a chat to the men from the wood mill.

They took a broom and some tools, and went to get the Big Bad Fox.

The Big Bad Fox ran and ran.

He ran until he was lost.

The Big Bad Fox cannot go back to the woods as he is too lost.

Jess scoops up her things, and skips to Nan's.

Nan likes her snack. "Thank you, Jess," she said.

Questions:

1. Why is Jess going to her Nan's?
2. How far is the walk?
3. Who does she see in the woods?
4. What does she do?
5. Do you think Jess is safe now? Why or why not?

Roof Top

Written by Kassi Gilmour

Practise the sounds

u l ll ss ff b j w wh y

th sh v qu z zz x

ch ng oo oo th

Practise blending sounds

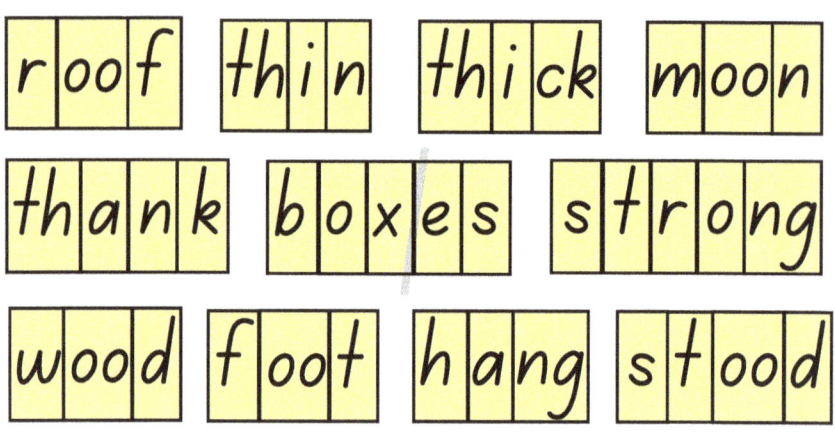

Practise tricky words

to on<u>to</u> they of are have all her

day for like said what want saw

be were one some come

Roof Top
Set 5

Written by Kassi Gilmour

I am Chad. This is my van.

My roof is thin. Dad said that we cannot hop on the roof.

Bill's roof is thick and strong.
He can hop up onto his roof.

Bill likes to sit on the roof to look at the moon.

The moon is big.

One day, I saw Bill's foot hang from his roof.

"Help!" Bill said.

I ran to my dad and said, "Bill is stuck on his roof. Can we help?"

"Yes!" said Dad. He ran to the back shed to get some thick, wood boxes.

"Hold on!" Dad said to Bill.

Dad stacks the wood boxes like steps.

"Let go, Bill," Dad said. Bill let go and fell onto the top box.

Bill stood still. "Thank you," he said to my dad.

Dad let Bill have the boxes.

"I think I will sit on the boxes and not on the roof," Bill tells Dad.

The next day, Bill and I sat on the wood boxes to look at the moon.

Questions:

1. What is Chad's roof like?
2. How is Bill's roof different?
3. Was it safe for Bill to climb up on his roof?
4. How did Chad's dad help Bill?
5. Do you have a favourite spot to look at the night sky?

Zoo

Written by Kassi Gilmour

Practise the sounds

u l ll ss ff b j w wh y
th sh v qu z zz x
ch ng oo oo th

Practise blending sounds

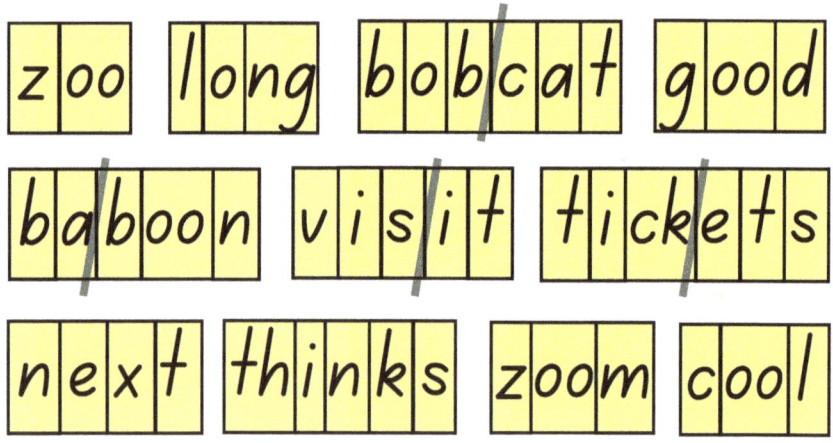

Practise tricky words

to into they of are have all her
day for like said what want saw
be were one some come

Zoo

Set 5

Written by Kassi Gilmour

It is a long trip to the zoo. I like the zoo, but not the long trip.

Mum, Dad, Pat and I get on the bus to the tram stop.

Then, we hop on the tram that travels to the zoo.

Dad has some cash and gets the tickets.

I want to visit the crocs.

Dad wants to zoom to the baboons.

Mum wants to stroll to the sloths.

Pam gets a map. She plans a track for us to look at all of them.

"Off to the bobcats," said Pam.

They are quick and can hunt. They have black spots and look soft.

Next, we look at all the frogs.

Some are big and some are small.

Then, we stroll to the fox den.

Foxes are small and look a bit like dogs.

I am glad that the crocs are next.

The crocs are long and can swim. They snap at food.

The Baboons are next, and dad stands still to look.

"When will we look at the sloths?" Mum quizzes Pat.

"Soon," Pat tells her mum.

Soon, we get a good look at the sloths. Mum thinks sloths are cool. I think they are slack.

At the end of the day, we go back on the tram and bus.

It was a long day, but it was a good day at the zoo.

Questions:

1. Who is going to the zoo?
2. How do they get there?
3. Why does Pat map out a path for the family to follow?
4. What animals did they see at the zoo?
5. Have you ever been to a zoo? If so, what animals did you like?

Pool

Written by Kassi Gilmour

Practise the sounds

u l ll ss ff b j w wh y
th sh v qu z zz x
ch ng oo oo th

Practise blending sounds

| p | oo | l | | l | oo | k | | c | oo | l | | f | oo | d |

| B | e | th | | l | u | n | ch | | w | i | sh | e | s |

| th | i | n | k | s | | ch | a | t | | f | i | n | i | sh |

Practise tricky words

in<u>to</u> they of are have all her day
for like said what want saw be
were one some come

Pool

Set 5

Written by Kassi Gilmour

One hot day, Beth and Zack went to cool off at the pool.

"I like to swim," said Beth.
"I like to jump and flip," Zack said.

Beth was quick to swim some laps of the pool.

Zack flips off the blocks into the pool.

They look at the clock and stop for lunch.

"What food do you have?" Zack said to Beth.

"I have a ham bun," Beth said.

Zack looks at his lunch and wishes that he had a ham bun. He thinks his lunch is yuck.

When they finish lunch,
they sit and chat for a bit.

Soon, it was 2 o'clock. Beth said, "Come on, Zack. Let's swim one lap as quick as we can."

Beth and Zack swim one lap.

Then, they had to pack up.

"What a good day to spend at the pool," Zack tells Beth.

Questions:

1. Why are Beth and Zack going to the pool?
2. What does Beth like to do?
3. What does Zack like to do?
4. Do Beth and Zack like their lunches? How do you know?
5. What would you like to do at the pool?

www.ingramcontent.com/pod-product-compliance
Lightning Source LLC
Chambersburg PA
CBHW042131100526
44587CB00026B/4259